All About Animals / Todo sobre los animales

What's an INSECT?
¿Qué es un INSECTO?

Anna Kaspar

Traducción al español:
Eduardo Alamán

PowerKiDS press

New York

Published in 2012 by The Rosen Publishing Group, Inc.
29 East 21st Street, New York, NY 10010

Copyright © 2012 by The Rosen Publishing Group, Inc.

All rights reserved. No part of this book may be reproduced in any form without permission in writing from the publisher, except by a reviewer.

First Edition

Editor: Amelie von Zumbusch
Book Design: Ashley Drago

Traducción al español: Eduardo Alamán

Photo Credits: Cover © www.iStockphoto.com/Anyka; pp. 5, 10, 13, 18, 21, 24 (caterpillar, luna moth) Shutterstock.com; pp. 6, 24 (antennae) © www.iStockphoto.com/Imagedepotpro; p. 9 iStockphoto/Thinkstock; pp. 14, 24 (wasp) © www.iStockphoto.com/Arman Davtyan; p. 17 John Foxx/Stockbyte/Thinkstock; p. 22 Brian Gordon Green/Getty Images.

Library of Congress Cataloging-in-Publication Data

Kaspar, Anna.
 [What's an insect? Spanish & English]
 What's an insect? = ¿Qué es un insecto? / by Anna Kaspar. — 1st ed.
   p. cm. — (All about animals = Todo sobre los animales)
 Includes index.
 ISBN 978-1-4488-6704-2 (library binding)
 1. Insects—Juvenile literature. I. Title. II. Title: ¿Qué es un insecto?
 QL467.2.K36618 2012
 595.7—dc23
                                                2011024006

Web Sites: Due to the changing nature of Internet links, PowerKids Press has developed an online list of Web sites related to the subject of this book. This site is updated regularly. Please use this link to access the list:
www.powerkidslinks.com/aaa/insect/

Manufactured in the United States of America

CPSIA Compliance Information: Batch #WW12PK: For Further Information contact Rosen Publishing, New York, New York at 1-800-237-9932

Contents / Contenido

So Many Insects 4
Insect Bodies 7
Many Kinds of Insects 12
Words to Know 24
Index 24

¡Cuántos insectos! 4
El cuerpo de los insectos 7
Muchos tipos de insectos 12
Palabras que debes saber..24
Índice..24

Insects are Earth's most common kind of animal.

Los insectos son el tipo de animal más común.

Insects have **antennae** on their heads. Insects sense things with their antennae.

Los insectos tienen **antenas** en la cabeza. Los insectos perciben cosas por medio de sus antenas.

Adult insects have six legs. Their bodies have three parts.

Los insectos adultos tienen seis patas. Sus cuerpos tienen tres partes.

Insects pass through stages as they grow. Butterflies start out as **caterpillars**.

Durante su crecimiento, los insectos pasan por diversas etapas. Las mariposas comienzan siendo **orugas**.

Ants live in groups called colonies. The members of a colony live and work together.

Las hormigas viven en grupos llamados colonias. Los miembros de las colonias viven y trabajan juntos.

Wasps often live in colonies, too. Most wasps eat other kinds of insects.

Con frecuencia, las **avispas** también viven en colonias. La mayoría de las avispas comen otros insectos.

Bees drink from flowers. Some bees dance to show other bees where to find flowers.

Las abejas chupan el jugo de las flores. Algunas abejas bailan para indicar a otras abejas dónde encontrar flores.

Flies use the hairs on their feet to taste things.

_____

Las moscas usan los pelos de sus patas para probar las cosas.

Luna moths live in North America. Females make a smell that draws males to them.

Las **polillas luna** viven en Norteamérica. Las polillas hembras producen un aroma que atrae a los machos.

Male crickets chirp. They rub their wings together to make noise.

Los grillos machos hacen un chirrido. Frotan sus alas para hacer ruido.

WORDS TO KNOW/ PALABRAS QUE DEBES SABER

 antennae/ (las) antenas

 caterpillar/ (la) oruga

 luna moth/ (la) polilla luna

 wasp/ (la) avispa

INDEX

C
colonies, 12, 15

K
kind(s), 4, 15

S
smell, 20
stages, 11

W
wasps, 15
wings, 23

ÍNDICE

A
alas, 23
aroma, 20
avispas, 15

C
colonias, 12, 15

E
etapas, 11

T
tipo(s), 4, 15